Endorsements for The Boaz Blessing

"In various seasons, the Holy Spirit highlights different portions of the Word of God to us personally and corporately. Ben Peters has done a great job of bringing us a now word from the book of Ruth and how favor with God can transform a life. Ben carries the fire of the Holy Spirit and yet anchors believers in the Word of Truth. I am sure you will be inspired thru this revelatory teaching."

James W. Goll, Encounters Network • Prayer Storm •
Compassion Acts, Best Selling Author,
Harvest International Ministries Apostolic Team

"Ben Peter's book, *The Boaz Blessing* will empower you to live in the blessed life that God ordained for you. It will fill you with faith and expectancy!"

Patricia King, Founder of XPmedia

"The story of Boaz and Ruth is one of hope. It fills you with faith and strength to press forward with expectancy that you too can be redeemed. Yet there is a whole other dimension in the book of Ruth that Ben brings to light – *The Boaz Blessing*. This little book gives you a powerful transforming prayer that will impact your life and those around you. It provides you with a framework on how to bless through the power of the word."

Dr. Ché Ahn, Senior Pastor, HROCK Church, Pasadena, CA President, Harvest International Ministry, International Chancellor, Wagner Leadership Institute

"This is a great book to read to encourage you to walk in favor, not shame. No matter where you have come from, your background or nationality, God has a plan for you. To walk in the blessings and the over- flow...then walk into the palace. *The Boaz Blessing* is a book of encouragement to see how God ordered Boaz, Ruth and Naomi's footsteps and to see where God led them and how He put them together. the book also shares with greater insight that God will take care of ALL your needs, just walk in His will."

Joan Hunter, President of Joan Hunter Ministries, Author, Evangelist, Apostle

"Having been blessed to personally walk through a modern day "Ruth and Naomi" preservation of life experience in Bethlehem, I can give testimony that Abba in still in the business of releasing His Kinsman Redeemer blessing upon those who honor, seek and trust Him. There is more than an abundance of bread in His house! As always, Papa Ben has brought revelation to the Word of God in a way that is transforming and empowering. He first shared this revelation with me when we were together in Bethlehem. It is such a blessing to see that it is now in written form to transform the world!"

"To speak a blessing is to change the world! Ben Peters has been doing this for years and seeing the fruit of changed lives and transformed communities wherever the seeds of blessing have found fertile soil. *The Boaz Blessing* is a revelation of the heart of our Father, from whom goodness and favor cascade in showers of pure love. This book can unlock overflowing reward and lasting favor for you and those you influence."

The Boaz Blessing:
Releasing the Power of this Ancient Blessing
into Your World Today

The Boaz Blessing

Releasing the Power of this Ancient Blessing into Your

World Today

Ben Peters

The Boaz Blessing
Releasing the Power of this Ancient Blessing into Your World Today

Published by Inscribe Press, LLC, Tigard, OR
Cover design by Pelton Media Group, LLC, Portland, OR

Cover Font: *"Hey August"* by Khurasan
www.dafont.com/hey-august.font

Unless otherwise indicated, Bible quotations are taken from the New King James Version. Copyright © 1983 by Thomas Nelson, Inc.

ISBN: 978-1-951611-01-9 (Hardback)
             978-1-951611-00-2 (Paperback)
Library of Congress Control Number: 2019915568

Learn more about Ben and Brenda Peters at
www.kingdomsendingcenter.org

Inscribe Press
Creativity Unleashed

Contents

Chapter 1

Words of Blessing

Woven into this tender and beautiful love story are several unique types of blessings.

I AM ALWAYS AMAZED when I miss something in Scripture that seems so obvious, because I have read it dozens of times before. That has been happening to me over and over again in this one short little book called Ruth. I know the basic story; I have known it since I was a young child, but I never saw this book as a book of blessings. Today, it's so obvious, I can't imagine missing it. Since I've never heard or read anything about this topic, in over sixty years as a Christian, I suspect that you have never caught this fact either. Woven into the tender and beautiful love story contained in the biblical account of Ruth are several unique types of blessings. This book will deal specifically with the Boaz Blessing, but we will look at some other important benedictions as well.

For several years there has been much teaching on the importance of speaking positive words and making positive confessions. The "positive speaking" message certainly has a biblical basis and for the most part, it has been a blessing to the church as we move towards the "restoration of all things" spoken of by Peter in Acts

3:21. We also hear quite often in our Kingdom journey regarding the power of word curses, especially as they relate to negative pronouncements over ourselves, such as, "I'm so stupid!" or "I can't do anything right."

Shifting our focus from ourselves to others is an important step for us to take as we move towards the goal of bringing the Kingdom of heaven to earth

More recently, there has been a growing interest in, and an increase in teaching about, the power of the blessing. This is a significant shift in the right direction. While the idea of making a positive confession focuses mostly on improving circumstances for the person doing the speaking, the idea of speaking blessings focuses mostly on releasing life and hope for someone else.

Shifting our focus from ourselves to others is a very important step for the church to take as we move towards the goal of bringing the Kingdom of heaven to the earth, where God's will shall be done here, just as it is there. I don't think I can make this point strongly enough, much less overstate it. We cannot, and will not, ever achieve the glory God wants us to demonstrate to the world until we become like Jesus in this way. His prayers were always focused on helping others, even when His needs were extreme. Remember His words from the cross, "Father, forgive them, for they know not what they do."

Also, "Woman, behold your son."

And "Son, behold your mother."

This shift is wonderful, because the more we focus

on others, the more blessed we also become. As we read Paul's words in Philippians about Jesus, who became the "Ultimate Servant," we are humbled and exhilarated by His example:

> *Therefore God also has highly exalted Him and has given Him the name which is above every name, that at the name of Jesus every knee should bow, of things in Heaven, and of those on earth, and of those under the earth, and that every tongue should confess that Jesus Christ is Lord, to the glory of God the Father. (Philippians 2:9-11)*

In Chapter Two we will examine three types of blessings in the book of Ruth, and then move into the main message of this little book in Chapter Three. I trust you will read through to the end, and I encourage you to not miss the powerful revelation that has touched so many lives already.

Chapter 2

Ruth–A Book of Blessings

*Releasing blessings expresses the heart of God,
and keeps us secure*

RUTH IS A LITERARY MASTERPIECE, a story of redemption from the time of Israel's judges, and a book of wonderful insight into releasing blessing. In this chapter, we will look at several benedictions that we discover in the biblical account. As noted in Chapter One, there are three main types of blessings found in Ruth. The first is the traditional spoken blessing such as, "The Lord bless you and keep you." The second is a statement of promise or covenant commitment to the other person. The third is an act of kindness which brings great comfort to the recipient.

Elimelech and Naomi

You probably remember how Ruth's story begins, but let's quickly review the setting. A man named Elimelech is living in Bethlehem in the land of Judah with his wife Naomi. They have two sons, Mahlon and Chilion. When devastating famine sweeps the region, the family pulls up stakes and moves to neighboring Moab.

But disaster strikes the family after arriving in Moab when Elimelech dies. Naomi's main source of security is gone, but she still has two sons, who take responsibility to care for her. She is comforted when her sons marry two Moabite gals, named Orpah and Ruth. But after ten years, once again Naomi is devastated by the deaths of both her sons, leaving her without a man in her life to take care of her in her old age.

Naomi Blesses Her Daughters-in-Law

Naomi decides to return to Bethlehem alone, and she exhorts her two daughters-in-law to return to their people and try to start a new life in Moab. The first blessing is recounted when Naomi blesses both Orpah and Ruth in Ruth 1:8,9,33.

> *"The Lord deal kindly with you as you have dealt with the dead and with me. The Lord grant that you may find rest, each in the house of her husband."*

Deeply moved, both daughters-in-law bless Naomi in return, by saying that they will go with her. Naomi insists that they need to stay in Moab and find husbands from their own people while they are still young, rather than going with her to an unfamiliar land, to live with an unfamiliar people.

Orpah reluctantly submits to Naomi's requests and says a tearful farewell, but Ruth will not change her mind, knowing that Naomi desperately needs a close friend in this most difficult transition time. Yes, Ruth had just lost her own husband, but she knows that Naomi has not just lost her husband, but has lost everyone in her life that should be there to take care of her in her old age. Ruth cannot and will not leave Naomi to fend for herself.

RUTH BLESSES NAOMI

> *But Ruth said, "Entreat me not to leave you, or to turn back from following after you. For wherever you go, I will go, and wherever you lodge, I will lodge; Your people shall be my people, and your God, my God. Where you die, I will die, and there will I be buried. The Lord do so to me, and more also, if anything but death parts you and me."*
> *(Ruth 1:16,17)*

This famous covenant has blessed people for three thousand years. More than fifty years ago, my Uncle Hank Kliever sang, "Wither Thou Goest, I Will Go" at my wedding, where my beloved Brenda and I made a covenant with each other; a covenant we have kept since that day, August 11, 1967.

If God is with us, we have a powerful Friend who will provide for and take care of us. That means that we are secure and blessed.

After speaking this unique covenant blessing over Naomi, Ruth joins her in her journey to Bethlehem, and upon their arrival, Naomi informs her old friends and relatives about her painful losses in the land of Moab. Obviously, they also learn that Ruth, the Moabitess, has made the journey with her mother-in-law.

BLESSING BY GLEANING

Driven by her love for Naomi and the need to provide for their physical needs, Ruth asks Naomi for permission to go out to the barley fields and glean what she can by following the harvesters. Ruth 2:3 declares that Ruth

> *"...happened to come to the part of the field belonging to Boaz, who was of the family of Elimelech."*

In other words, Boaz is a relative of Naomi's deceased husband.

BOAZ BLESSES HIS REAPERS

> *Now, behold, Boaz came from Bethlehem, and said to the reapers, "The Lord be with you!" (Ruth 2:4a)*

Instead of our typical greeting—"How are you doing?"—Boaz pronounces a blessing upon them. When someone says, "The Lord be with you," they are giving the ultimate blessing, since, if God is with us, we have a powerful Friend who will provide for and take care of us, and no one can harm us without His permission. That means that we are secure and blessed.

This blessing expresses the heart of Boaz and, as we will discover, the heart of many of the people of Bethlehem.

THE REAPERS BLESS BOAZ

> *And they answered him, "The Lord bless you!"*

Responding to the blessing from Boaz, the reapers are quick to respond with a blessing of their own. When they say, "The Lord bless you!" they are saying, "May you prosper and be filled with every good thing from God." It is interesting that we are accustomed to ending a letter or a friendly conversation with a "God bless you!" but apparently it was the Jewish custom to begin a conversation with such blessings.

Boaz Blesses Ruth (Ruth 2:11,12)

The next two chapters will deal with this amazing blessing in detail.

Naomi Blesses Boaz

After Ruth returns to Naomi with a shopping cart full of food from Boaz, Naomi speaks this blessing over Boaz:

"Blessed be he of the Lord, who has not forsaken His kindness to the living and to the dead!" (Ruth 2:20)

Here is another statement of blessing, asking God to bless the man for his kindness to Ruth and Naomi. In doing so, she also is giving thanks to God for not forsaking her in her time of need, as well as remembering her dead husband by taking care of his family.

Naomi Blesses Ruth

Naomi was a kind and thoughtful mother-in-law, who felt compassion for Ruth, just as Ruth had felt great compassion for her in coming to Bethlehem with her. She wanted to bless her with a better future and realized that God was providing a close relative to become an even greater blessing than he had already been. Naomi declares:

> *"My daughter, shall I not seek security for you, that it may be well with you?" (Ruth 3:1)*

With that introduction, Naomi proceeds to explain to Ruth how to send a message to Boaz that she is now a relative whom he can marry to produce seed for the house of Elimelech. The strategy sounds a little strange to our culture, and must have been a bit embarrassing to Ruth, but because she is submitted to Naomi, she is willing to go through with the unusual ritual.

BOAZ BLESSES RUTH AGAIN

One night, after Boaz has gone to sleep by a pile of threshed grain, Ruth quietly goes to the threshing floor and lies down at the feet of Boaz. Around midnight, Boaz wakes up, and to his surprise, he finds the young lady lying at his feet. She asks him to take her under his wing because he is a close relative. He responds with another amazing blessing for Ruth:

> *"Blessed are you of the Lord, my daughter! For you have shown more kindness at the end than at the beginning, in that you did not go after young men, whether poor or rich. And now, my daughter, do not fear, I will do for you all that you request, for all the people of my town know that you are a virtuous woman." (Ruth 3:10,11)*

After speaking these words, Boaz further blesses

Ruth with six ephahs of barley to take home to Naomi. In Boaz, we see a tremendous example of a man who loved to bless others, and he has often been cited as a type of Christ, in that, like Boaz, Jesus is our Kinsman Redeemer.

THE PEOPLE AND ELDERS AT THE GATE BLESS BOAZ AND RUTH

In an interesting ceremony at the town gates, Boaz declares that he is purchasing the land owned by Elimelech and at the same time, he is acquiring Ruth, the daughter-in-law of Elimelech, as his wife in order to perpetuate his relative's lineage, as proscribed according to the Law of Moses. Once he finishes his declaration, Boaz turns to the elders and people assembled and says to them, "You are witnesses this day."

What follows is a powerful prophetic blessing, released over Boaz and Ruth by those assembled:

And all the people who were at the gate and the elders, said, "We are witnesses. The Lord make the woman who is coming to your house like Rachel and Leah, the two who built the house of Israel; and may you prosper in Ephrathah and be famous in Bethlehem. May your house be like the house of Perez, whom Tamar bore to Judah, because of the offspring which the Lord will give you from this young woman." (Ruth 3:11,12).

This was truly an amazing prophetic blessing. What the people and elders spoke to Boaz literally came to pass. Boaz did become famous in Bethlehem, and his offspring, Obed, was the father of Jesse, the father of

King David, and was in the direct lineage of Jesus, who also was born in Bethlehem.

God Blesses Boaz and Ruth

Boaz takes Ruth to be his wife, and the Lord gives her conception and she bears a son. For any woman in Israel, giving birth to a son is a wonderful blessing, because her prime fulfillment in life comes from being able to present her husband with a male child to become his heir and perpetuate his family line on the earth.

Women of Bethlehem Bless the Lord and Naomi

The final blessing in this book of blessings comes from the women of Bethlehem as they give thanks to God and demonstrate their love and appreciation for both Naomi and Ruth (Ruth 4:14,15).

> *Then the women said to Naomi, '"Blessed be the Lord who has not left you this day without a close relative; and may his name be famous in Israel! And may he be to you a restorer of life and a nourisher of your old age; for your daughter-in-law, who loves you, who is better to you than seven sons, has borne him."*

What an amazing prophetic blessing declaration! In these two verses, the women of Judah are giving praise to God for His provision for Naomi, and also prophesying the future of the child which God has given to Boaz and Ruth. They bless him with being famous in Israel and declare him to be one who will nourish and care for Naomi in her old age.

Obed certainly did become famous in Israel, as he was the grandfather of the great king, David. Of course, because his name is mentioned in the Bible, he is also famous throughout the Christian world. Concerning becoming a person to nourish Naomi in her old age—the Bible doesn't tell us if that happened, but when you think of his parents and Naomi, it is hard to imagine that he was not a generous, unselfish, and compassionate young man.

One more little point. The name Obed was given to him by the women in Naomi's neighborhood. This was another prophetic act on their part. His name comes from a word that means worshipper. Is it not interesting that his grandson is the most famous worshipper in history? King David wrote the majority of the Psalms and invented many different instruments for worship; he hired thousands of singers and musicians to worship twenty-four seven in the tabernacle he had built for intimate adoration of his God.

When they say, "The Lord bless you!" they are saying, "May you prosper and be filled with every good thing from God."

What blesses me as much as anything else is that those who prophesied to Naomi about Obed were just unnamed neighbor women. They were not Samuel or Nathan or Gad or any other high-ranking prophet. They were people like you and me who rejoiced in the blessings which had come to a friend who had suffered much loss in times past, but now was receiving the rewards of trusting God through it all.

Chapter 3

The Boaz Blessing
(Part 1)

God sees our actions differently than we do...

IN THE SECOND CHAPTER of Ruth, we read about the young Moabite woman going to glean wherever she could, with the permission of Naomi. As we know, she found herself in the field of Boaz, without any idea who he was at the time. When Boaz saw her, he asked his workers about her, since she was a stranger to him. They shared with him the story of how she came to Bethlehem with Naomi after the death of her husband and both her sons.

Boaz quickly walked up to Ruth and spoke the following words:

> *"You will listen, my daughter, will you not? Do not go to glean in another field, nor go from here, but stay close by my young women. Let your eyes be on the field which they reap, and go after them. Have I not commanded the young men not to touch you? And when you are thirsty, go to the vessels and drink from what the young men have drawn." (Ruth 2:8,9).*

Ruth was overwhelmed by the kindness of this

man, who must have been significantly older than she. Her response, as a foreigner, could be understood, knowing the culture of her day. Notice Ruth's humble heart in the following narrative:

> *"So she fell on her face, bowed down to the ground, and said to him, 'Why have I found favor in your eyes, that you should take notice of me, since I am a foreigner?'"*

RUTH KNEW WHY SHE WAS NOT WORTHY OF FAVOR

Almost every Christian can identify with Ruth in this story. We all know many reasons why we are not worthy of God's favor. Guilt, shame, and condemnation attach to our souls like bloodsuckers, causing us to hide in the shadows, almost hoping God doesn't notice us.

Almost every Christian can identify with Ruth in this story. We all know many reasons why we are not worthy of God's favor.

So many Christians think that if they can just make it through those pearly gates, they will be content. Finding favor with God requires that they present themselves before Him, and this is not something they feel comfortable doing.

In addition to the above negative feelings, we often struggle with a deep sense of inferiority in many areas, along with the apparent lack of significant accomplishments on our resumes. We just don't believe there is any reason we would find favor with God. We may also feel unworthy because of our race or skin color, or a lack of education, money, or talents.

Certainly, Ruth suffered from feelings of unworthiness due to her nationality. It was normal to be treated as inferior if you were in a foreign country. I often notice immigrants from other nations, including Latinos, Asians, and Europeans remaining low-key in the presence of others, not wanting to draw attention to themselves. For some it may be a matter of not having legal documents, but for most it's just a lack of confidence that they will be accepted. Yes, it's true. Most of us know all the reasons why we don't deserve special favor. The good news is that there is a special Someone who has a different opinion.

Boaz, the Type of Christ

Many theologians have referred to Boaz as the "Kinsman Redeemer." This relates to the process by which Boaz would take Ruth to be his wife, according to the Jewish culture and the Law of Moses.

I would like you to reflect on the following words of Boaz to Ruth and apply them to yourself as if they were the words of Jesus to you. If you can receive them, I believe God will touch your heart and transform your relationship with Him.

Boaz Knew Why She Was Worthy of Favor

Boaz answered Ruth's sincere question with the following:

"It has been fully reported to me all that you have done for your mother-in-law since the death of

> *your husband, and how you have left your father and your mother and the land of your birth, and have come to a people whom you did not know before." (Ruth 2:11).*

Now, I'm sure that most of you don't have a mother-in-law named Naomi, but don't let that rob you of a blessing from this story. Let's take the first few words and then apply them to your own story. Listen to the voice of the Holy Spirit, speaking for the Lord as He says, "It has been fully reported to Me all that you have done for ..." Jesus got the memo regarding the sacrifices you have made for your own family and friends, and even those who don't love you. You may think your contribution to others is insignificant; so did Ruth! But God sees things differently than you.

He knows the times you set down your own ambitions to help someone else fulfill theirs. Most people remember the classic movie, "It's a Wonderful Life," starring Jimmy Stewart. He too had a negative opinin of his own self-worth and tried to take his life. In the story, an angel named Clarence rescued him and showed him what a difference his life had made by showing him what would have happened if he had not ever lived.

Many people would greatly benefit from such an experience, but that's probably not going to happen in real life. However, please understand that God made you for a wonderful purpose and He has planned a wonderful life for you.

He has noticed your humble heart and your servant

spirit. He hasn't forgotten when you went out of your way to help someone in need; when you used your creative talents to make a special gift; when you prayed for a sick child or visited folks at the nursing home; when you sacrificed your finances for someone with a greater need than yours.

Friends, Jesus got the memo. It's all been recorded and your good deeds have not been forgotten. No matter how guilty you feel about your negative actions, there is still a record of the positive, sacrificial deeds that you dismissed as something that "anyone would do." The fact is: not everyone would have done what you did. You have a way of going beyond the expected to do the things that others would forget.

Yes, no matter how hard you try to hide in the shadows of others, Jesus knows everything you have done for Him and for His kids. And He is extremely grateful. What you have done for the least of His kids is as if you did it specifically for Him.

WE'RE TALKING ABOUT FAVOR, NOT SALVATION

Lest anyone think we are saying we can earn our salvation, we hasten to assure you that we are talking about something totally different. We know that we can do nothing to earn our salvation. That has already been earned by Jesus' sacrifice on the cross. But we are clearly told that we will be rewarded according to our works when Jesus returns. (Rev. 22:12).

Favor is different than salvation. Favor is when something moves the heart of God, or a person with authority, to show special kindness beyond the normal. When we have God's favor, things go better than we expected, even though we may have just gone through a deep, dark valley, like Naomi had.

RECEIVE SO THAT YOU CAN GIVE

My prayer is that you will totally receive the truth that God believes that you deserve favor, despite your failures and weaknesses. Because you have responded to the promptings and wooing of the Holy Spirit, you have touched other's lives and blessed them on behalf of Jesus.

Once you accept this truth for yourself, it's time to begin to look around at others who need to believe it as well. They are everywhere around you and they all need to be aware that their sacrifices have been reported to God in heaven, who is their Creator and Father, and He eagerly wants to be their Friend. God wants to use you to impact them with this truth, which leads us to the second part of the Boaz Blessing.

Chapter 4

The Boaz Blessing
(Part 2)

The heart of the Blessing:
"The Lord repay your work..."

AS WE LEARNED in Chapter Three, God "received the memo" regarding our sacrifice on behalf of His Kingdom and the people He died for. In this chapter, we will address the subject of what action God will take with this information, and how to confer this wonderful blessing upon others.

Boaz did not just acknowledge that he had heard about what Ruth had done for Naomi. He spoke a prophetic blessing over her life and then began to cooperate with God in assisting this prophetic blessing to come to pass.

The very heart of this wonderful Boaz Blessing is contained in the words Boaz spoke to Ruth.

"The Lord repay your work and a full reward be given you by the Lord God of Israel under whose wings you have come for refuge." (Ruth 2:12)

WAGES

The first part of this blessing is, "The Lord repay your work." This speaks to me of wages, which we earn by working for the King. Certainly, the King can afford to pay His employees, and He is not going to give them the minimum wage. Rather, He is a very kind and generous employer, and although some of our benefits may be literally "out of this world," we accept the promise of Jesus that also "in this life" we will receive wages for our service to Him (Mark 10:29-30).

UNCLAIMED BENEFITS

I'm reminded of the promises in Psalm 103. We are told by David not to forget all God's benefits. God is the one who forgives all our sins and heals all our diseases. The list of benefits goes on and on. But it's like some of the benefits we get from our jobs or from the government. Many of them require that we apply for them.

Our King is a kind and generous employer. His benefits are literally "out of this world"

Decades ago, Brenda and I worked for a few years in Canada. Having lived in the USA since 1975, we never thought of the fact that we might qualify for benefits due us. Fortunately, someone mentioned something about it and while ministering in Saskatchewan, we went to a government office to inquire. Sure enough, we had benefits coming. We had already missed a year or two by that time, but today we enjoy a little extra cash each month because we applied for the benefits that Canada provides for its workers.

In the case of Ruth, she was unaware of any benefits or even wages coming to her, so Boaz made the application for her by speaking this blessing over her.

I am convinced the Holy Spirit is anointing this word right now as I write. I speak this blessing of wages over you, and declare that your work will produce the wages you have earned from the King of kings. But more than that, I declare and decree that God would make you like Boaz. You will recognize the labor and sacrifice of others and you will make application for them to obtain the wages that they have earned. You will find that the more you speak this blessing over others, the more you will also be blessed. The second half of this part of the blessing is similar but with additional meaning.

A Full Reward

The statement "A full reward be given you," takes this blessing to a higher level. The word, "re- ward" means more than just wages. A reward implies honor and recognition, in addition to financial blessing. I believe that Boaz wanted Ruth to not only receive wages for her labor, but also to be honored and recognized by all his community for the amazing degree of love and compassion she had demonstrated to Naomi.

This may be hard for many to receive. To get paid for labor is one thing, but to be put in the spotlight and have people tell us how special we are would make many people quite uncomfortable. They would say, "Just slip my check under the door or put it in my mailbox so I can pay my bills, but don't make me take the stage and have everyone look at me."

But God doesn't want us to keep hiding in the shadows. He is our proud Papa, and He wants to show us off and brag about His children. So shake off the inferiority complex and allow God to show you how much He loves you and let Him honor you with a full reward—not a small reward, but a full reward.

Why is this important? If we don't allow Him to show us off and honor us, we are robbing Him of one of His greatest joys. In addition, if we don't accept that honor, it will be hard to sincerely bestow it on others. We want to be like Him and serve others like He did. We want to proclaim and declare that God is ready and willing to put the crown on our heads and the trophy in our hands for the labor we have performed for His glory. And of course, we want to be able to confer these honors upon others as well.

The last part of the blessing says, "The Lord God of Israel, under whose wings you have come for refuge." This speaks clearly to the fact that, because she forsook the gods of her family and nation and found refuge in her new adopted land, the God of Israel would honor her and protect her from harm.

When we forsake the other gods in our lives such as money, popularity, pleasure, etc., and seek first and foremost the Kingdom of God, the Lord honors and favors us in special ways. When we really trust the Lord with our lives and serve Him with all our hearts, He delights in bestowing honor.

Chapter 5

Favor After Favor

*God desires to bless you more than
you can possibly imagine*

WHEN BOAZ FINISHED what we are calling the "Boaz Blessing," Ruth's immediate response was:

> *"Let me find favor in your sight, my lord; for you have comforted me, and have spoken kindly to your maidservant, though I am not like one of your maidservants." (Ruth 2:13).*

This response is a little surprising, since Ruth had just asked Boaz why she found favor in his sight. Then Boaz responded with the Boaz Blessing, telling her why she had found favor. Now Ruth is asking for more favor.

What Ruth goes on to say is that "because you have comforted me and spoken kindly to me, I want to take advantage of your kindness by asking for a little more favor, even though I still feel like I don't deserve it." Ruth is well aware of her lowly condition in the society because of her poverty and because she is a minority person in Israel. She is also aware of the need of her mother-in-law, Naomi, who still has no one else but her to provide for her. So, when a man of the stature of Boaz shows her comfort and kindness, she cannot help but express both appreciation and her need for even more favor.

This story reminds me so much of the story of Moses on Mount Sinai with the Lord. God was very angry with Israel for having made a golden calf to worship as their god of deliverance. He told Moses that He would not go with them into the Promised Land but would just send an angel to conquer the land for them.

Moses interceded and argued with God until He relented and said:

> *"I will also do this thing that you have spoken; for you have found grace in My sight, and I know you by name." (Exodus 33:17)*

This was a huge turnaround for Moses and Israel. Moses had found grace (or favor) in God's sight, and He agreed to Moses' request. But look what Moses says after this amazing show of God's favor:

> *"Please, show me Your glory." (Exodus 33:18).*

This reminds me of the way all children behave. There are things they won't ask their parents until they have evidence that they are in a really good mood. If the parents say yes to one thing, that's a good time for children to request the bigger thing that they have been afraid to seek. Moses had never presented this request to God before, as far as we know, but he asked right after God answered "Yes," to his request for His presence to travel with them into the Promised Land.

And God granted the second request! In the same way, Ruth asked for more favor right after receiving favor. The response of Boaz was even more amazing. He didn't rebuke her for being greedy. Rather, he proceeded to provide more and more favor to her.

The following passage shows the increased favor she was given by Boaz:

> *Now Boaz said to her at mealtime, "Come here, and eat of the bread, and dip your piece of bread in the vinegar." So she sat beside the reapers, and he passed parched grain to her; and she ate and was satisfied, and kept some back. And when she rose up to glean, Boaz commanded his young men, saying, 'Let her glean even among the sheaves, and do not reproach her. Also let grain from the bundles fall purposely for her; leave it that she may glean, and do not rebuke her.'" (Ruth 2:14-16).*

Instead of being left to herself at mealtime, which would have been the norm for gleaners, she sat at the table with Boaz and his reapers. He himself passed her parched grain and gave her bread and invited her to dip it in the vinegar. She was able to eat until she was full and still have some left over to take to Naomi.

The application is simple: Don't be shy in asking God for more!

In addition, Boaz instructed his reapers to make it easier for her to glean by dropping grain intentionally for her to pick up. This would be a tremendous blessing to both Ruth and Naomi, and truly Ruth was finding even more favor with Boaz after she had asked for it.

The application is very simple. Don't be shy in asking for more. You won't get punished like Oliver Twist. God will be delighted to give you more, since He can see that you now believe that His is a loving God and His desire is to bless you more than you ever realized before.

The exciting thing about this is that once you have experienced the amazing grace of your God, you will be ready to enthusiastically share this truth with others, who need to understand God's great love.

Let's go from favor to favor and from glory to glory. It's only the lies of the enemy that hold us back. God is waiting with a big "YES," but we must ask. James declares,

> *"You do not have because you do not ask."*
> *(James 4:2)*

Chapter 6

❧

Sharing the Boaz Blessing

*God will give you more favor than you think you deserve,
and in turn, you can bless others!*

I TRUST THAT YOU are able to personally digest and apply the Boaz Blessing to your own life. It is a simple truth that God keeps track of your good deeds, while forgiving the bad things you do as soon as you repent. He will not ignore your sacrifices and service to Him and His children. He will give you much more favor than you think you deserve, and after He has shown you favor, He wants to give you even more, and He wants you to ask for it. In this final chapter, I want to encourage and exhort you to embrace the Boaz Blessing to the point where you can repeat it and adapt it to anyone God brings across your path. We will try to make it as simple and transferrable as possible, so you can use it in a multitude of different circumstances.

Let's lay out the basic framework of the Boaz Blessing and you can flesh it out with any details that the Lord puts on your heart or in your mind. You can always start with the same opening and then adapt the rest of your blessing to the person's particular circumstances. I believe that if you do this, you will find that people will be touched and changed for God's glory.

Here then is the simple essence of the Boaz Blessing:

1. It has been fully reported to God what you have done for Him and others.
2. May God repay you for your labor.
3. May a full reward be given you.
4. God wants you to ask for favor, because He is ready to give it to you.

Now here is a sample of how you could flesh it out for a particular individual: "God says that He knows all about the many sacrifices you have made for Him. It's all been written down in His book. Yes, He got all the memos from the angels He has assigned to you.

"He is going to give you the wages you have coming to you because you have been working faithfully for Him. And, by the way, God does not pay minimum wage. He is a very generous employer.

"In addition, may God honor and richly reward you for serving people behind the scenes, where you didn't get any recognition; doing tasks such as taking care of babies and little children who never thought of thanking you for anything. God plans on recognizing you in front of others. He will give honor to whom honor is due, and He says that you do deserve honor.

"Oh yes, I understand you think you don't deserve His favor because you have failed Him too many times. Well, guess what? You've asked for forgiveness and He has forgotten all those things, so He doesn't know what you're talking about.

"Finally, dear friend of Jesus, He wants you to ask

for more favor. He has already begun to show it to you, but He is waiting for you to ask for more, because He has a lot more where that came from; He just needs you to ask for it. He loves you more than you comprehend and He longs to show you just how much He enjoys blessing someone like you."

I humbly pray that God will use this simple blessing to enable you to be an even greater blessing to those in your life. May God anoint you and the message of this small book as you transfer the Boaz Blessing to those in your sphere of influence.

May wounded Christians arise and fulfill their destiny. May weary warriors receive encouragement to rejoin the battle. May non-believers become strong believers, and may everyone who reads this book know and understand in a new way that God longs to show His love and appreciation for every deed of kindness, whether small or great.

Appendix: Additional Biblical Examples

I WOULD GUESS that the books written on the power of our words would number well into the thousands, while the sermons preached on the subject could have reached the millions by now. (I am confident that no one can prove me wrong, because no one keeps track of such things.)

It is important that as the people of God, we learn to speak positive things about ourselves, and do not curse ourselves with unbiblical negativity and condemnation. Below are some examples from Scripture of the power our words contain.

WHY YOUR WORDS HAVE POWER

While some may scoff at the idea that what you say can really make a difference in your own life or the lives of others, we know from Scripture that it really is true for any believer in Jesus. We discover a key phrase mentioned several places in Isaiah as well as Jeremiah, while the concept is also clear in numerous places in the New Testament.

ISAIAH

The key Old Testament phrase is, "My Words in Your Mouths." God told Isaiah to tell the people that He had put His words in their mouths in order to establish the heavens, to lay the foundations of the earth, and to say to Zion, "You are My people" (Isaiah 51:16).

Think of the fact that God created everything we see as well as all that we don't see with the words of His mouth. It's incredible to think that He could put that kind of creative energy into the words we speak by putting His own words in our mouths. Whatever He means by establishing the heavens and laying the foundations of the earth, that same creative activity will be performed by us speaking His words. Some of us speculate that we will help God create the new heaven and the new earth, when He puts His own creative words in our mouths.

Isaiah 59:21 declares that God has made a covenant with His people, declaring, "My Spirit who is upon you, and My words which I have put in your mouth, shall not depart from your mouth, nor from the mouth of your descendants, nor from the mouth of your descendants' descendants, says the LORD, from this time and forevermore."

That sounds like something we can identify with, seeing it is a "forevermore" covenant. Notice the quote begins with "My Spirit, who is upon you." This is directly before the statement in which He declares that He has put His words in our mouths and that they will be in the mouths of our children and future descendants forever. Since we have once again embraced the concept of the Holy Spirit coming "upon us," we feel confident that God can still put words in our mouths.

JEREMIAH

Moving on to Jeremiah, we find a most profound statement by God to a young man who felt utterly unqualified for the assignment that God was giving him. God told the young prophet that he was not to be afraid, because He was putting His own words in Jeremiah's mouth. Then God followed that statement with this amazing declaration: "See, I have this day set you over the nations and over the kingdoms, to root out and to pull down, to destroy and to throw down, to build and to plant." (Jeremiah 1:10)

Thus, the words that God put in Jeremiah's mouth were powerful words--words that would give him authority over political leaders and kingdoms. He was to use God's words to tear down everything the enemy had built and root out what the enemy had planted. Then Jeremiah was to build God's Kingdom and plant seeds of righteousness in the earth. Once again, we see the amazing power of the words that God puts in our mouths.

NEW TESTAMENT

The New Testament also has many references to the power of our words and the fact that God can put His words in our mouth. Jesus complimented Peter for his declaration that Jesus was the Christ, saying that God had revealed it to him before Peter spoke the words. Jesus, Himself, declared that even He only spoke the words that He heard His Father speak.

I PETER

In his letter to the churches, Peter makes a profound

statement in I Peter 4:11: "If any man speaks, let him speak as the oracle of God." This not only informs us that God can put His words in our mouths; it is a command to speak His words rather than our own. Although Peter, himself, had trouble keeping this command in every circumstance, he had been greatly used of God on many occasions when he did, indeed, speak as the oracle of God.

One of those occasions is found in Acts 2, after the Holy Spirit came upon the one-hundred-and-twenty in the upper room. Peter preached a spontaneous message, quoting the Old Testament prophecy from Joel, about the pouring out of God's Spirit in the last days. When Peter finished preaching, three thousand souls were added to the church. On other occasions, he spoke up with great boldness when confronted by the rulers of the Jews, challenging them as to whether the apostles should obey God or men.

In Acts 3, Peter used words God put in his mouth to tell the crippled man at the temple gate to "rise up and walk." Clearly, Peter knew the power of speaking as an oracle of God and he wanted all Christians to experience that power. Remember, he said, "If *any* man speaks, let him speak as the oracle of God. He didn't say, "If an apostle speaks," but "If any man speaks." Peter is clearly teaching that God can put His words in your mouth. This is powerfully encouraging to me and should also be to you!

About the Author

Ben Peters has been a student of the Word all his life with a heritage of parents and grandparents living by faith and serving God. After formal ministry training in a Canadian seminary, he spent nearly 30 years in pastoral ministry, before transitioning to a mobile ministry with his wife, Brenda. They traveled nationally and internationally, teaching and encouraging the body of Christ with prophetic insight. They first traveled under the name, "Open Heart Ministries" and later established a ministry in Illinois called "Kingdom Sending Center." Ben has received many significant revelations and insights to awaken and activate the body of Christ around the world. *The Boaz Blessing* has become one of the most loved.

www.kingdomsendingcenter.org

ohmint@gmail.com

P.O. Box 25

Genoa, IL 60135

Other Books by Ben Peters

The Marriage Annointing: Meeting Marriage Challenges Head On with the Power of the Fruit and the Gifts of the Holy Spirit

With Me: A Captivating Journey into Intimacy

The Ultimate Convergence: An End Times Prophecy of the Greatest Shock and Awe Display Ever to Hit Planet Earth

Humility and How I Almost Achieved It: Uncovering a Highly Undervalued Key to Lasting Success and Kingdom Power

Resurrection: A Manual for Raising the Dead

Folding Five Ministries into One Powerful Team: Taking the Prophetic And Apostolic Reformation To The Next Powerful Level

The Kingdom-Building Church: Experiencing the Explosive Potential of the Church in Kingdom-Building Mode

Kings and Kingdoms: Anointing a New Generation of Kings to Serve the King of Kings

God's Favorite Number: The Secret Keys and Awesome Power of True Unity

Prophetic Ministry: Strategic Key to the Harvest

Faith on Fire: Dismantling Structures of Unbelief, Building Unshakeable Strongholds of Faith

Go Ahead, Be So Emotional: Empowering the Emotional Personality To do Awesome Exploits for God

Finding Your Place on Your Kingdom Mountain: A Practical Guide and Workbook for Reigning as Kings in the Kingdom of God

Holy How?: Holiness, the Sabbath, Communion and Baptism

Holy Passion ~ Desire on Fire: Igniting the Torch of Godly Passion

Finding Your Place on Your Mountain: A Practical Guide and Workbook for Reigning as Kings in the Kingdom of God

A Mandate to Laugh: Overcoming the Sennacherib Spirit

Signs and Wonders ~ To Seek or Not to Seek: Exploring the Power of the Miraculous to Bring People to Faith in God

Catching Up to the Third World: Seven Indispensable Keys to Explosive Revival in the Western Church

Birthing the Book Within You: Inspiration and Practical Help to Produce Your Own Book

Veggie Village and the Great & Dangerous Jungle: An Allegory

Available from Amazon
or email: ohmint@gmail.com